Brands We Know

American Girl

By Sara Green

Jump into the cockpit and take flight with Pilot books. Your journey will take you on high-energy adventures as you learn about all that is wild, weird, fascinating, and fun!

This edition first published in 2017 by Bellwether Media, Inc.

No part of this publication may be reproduced in whole or in part without written permission of the publisher.
For information regarding permission, write to Bellwether Media, Inc.,
Attention: Permissions Department,
5357 Penn Avenue South, Minneapolis, MN 55419.

Library of Congress Cataloging-in-Publication Data

Names: Green, Sara, 1964- author.
Title: American Girl / by Sara Green.
Description: Minneapolis, MN : Bellwether Media, Inc., 2017. | Series: Pilot:
    Brands We Know | Grades 3-8. | Includes bibliographical references and index.
Identifiers: LCCN 2016032040 (print) | LCCN 2016046495 (ebook) | ISBN
    9781626175532 (hardcover : alk. paper) | ISBN 9781681033006 (ebook)
Subjects: LCSH: American Girl (Firm)--Juvenile literature. | Dolls--United
    States--History--Juvenile literature. | Doll industry--United
    States--History--Juvenile literature.
Classification: LCC HD9993.D654 A445 2017 (print) | LCC HD9993.D654 (ebook)
  | DDC 338.7/68872210973--dc23
LC record available at https://lccn.loc.gov/2016032040

Editor: Christina Leighton   Designer: Josh Brink

Printed in the United States of America, North Mankato, MN.

Table of Contents

What Is American Girl?

A large party room is filled with bright decorations. Red paper stars dangle from the lights. Cupcakes and cookies are frosted in pink. The table is set with red plates and napkins. It is an American Girl birthday party! The guests arrive, each with an American Girl doll. Soon, the girls are laughing and playing. Even the dolls seem to have fun!

American Girl, formerly Pleasant Company, makes the American Girl **brand** of products. It has been part of a larger toy company, Mattel, Inc., since 1998. The American Girl **headquarters** is in Middleton, Wisconsin. The company makes dolls and **accessories**. It publishes books and the *American Girl* magazine. Some American Girl characters are also featured in movies. Kids and adults around the world recognize the company's star **logo**. American Girl has won more than 300 awards for its toys, programs, and best-selling books. Today, it is among the most popular doll brands in the United States!

By the Numbers

more than
153 million
American Girl books sold
since 1986

over
80 million
people have visited
American Girl stores
over time

more than
$100 million
in products and money
given to charities

about
2,300
employees

more than
52 million
web site visits
each year

more than
300
awards won over time

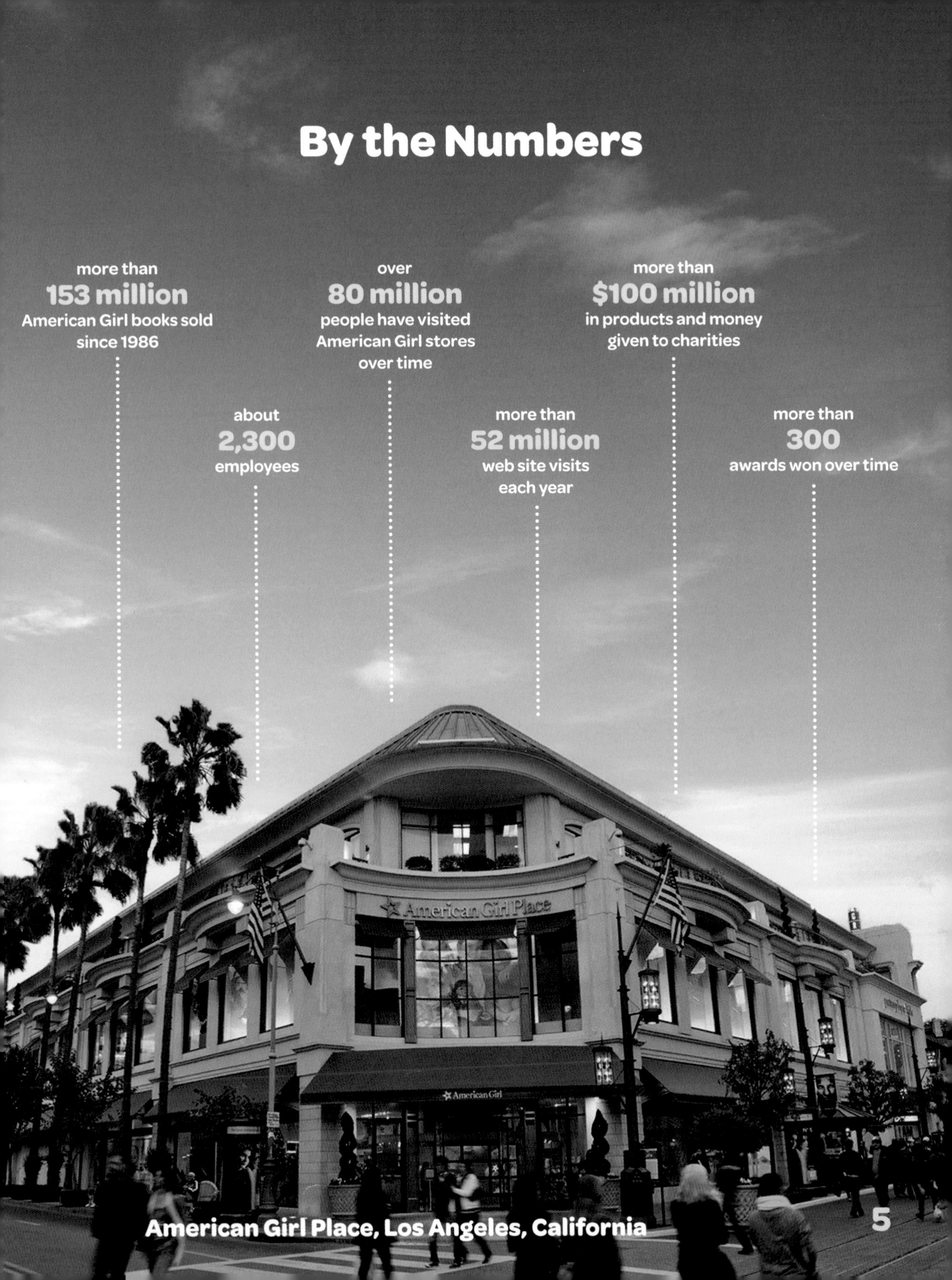

American Girl Place, Los Angeles, California

A Pleasant Beginning

The **founder** of American Girl is a woman named Pleasant Rowland. In the mid-1980s, Pleasant wanted to buy dolls for her nieces. She searched for dolls that looked like young girls. However, she only found dolls that looked like babies or teenagers. Pleasant decided to make her own dolls. A trip to **Colonial** Williamsburg, Virginia, inspired her to make historical dolls. She hoped girls would enjoy playing with the dolls and learning about history at the same time.

In 1986, she used her savings to start Pleasant Company in Middleton, Wisconsin. The first year, the company made three dolls set in different time periods. Kirsten Larson was from Minnesota in the 1850s, and Samantha Parkington lived in New York in the early 1900s. Molly McIntire was from Illinois in the 1940s. She lived during World War II. The dolls were made to be 18 inches (46 centimeters) tall. They looked like girls between the ages of 8 and 11. Book series, clothes, and accessories helped bring their stories to life.

A Great Place to Work

Warehouse workers wore mittens to pack orders when Pleasant Company first started. They sometimes did not have heat! Today, the company's headquarters has a gym, library, café, and toy store!

Molly McIntire

Many people doubted that Pleasant could find success selling historical dolls. However, she believed in her idea and did not give up. In the beginning, American Girl dolls were only sold through the mail. The company sent 500,000 American Girl catalogs to people around the country during its first year. People loved the look and history of the dolls. The dolls' stories were interesting and exciting. Soon, orders began pouring in. American Girl products earned $1.7 million in sales between September and December of 1986! A year later, the company introduced historical fashions for girls. Girls and their dolls could now wear matching clothes!

Kaya

Kaya's Smile

Kaya is a member of the Nez Perce tribe in the 1760s. Unlike the other dolls, Kaya's smile does not show her teeth. In her tribe, showing one's teeth is considered rude.

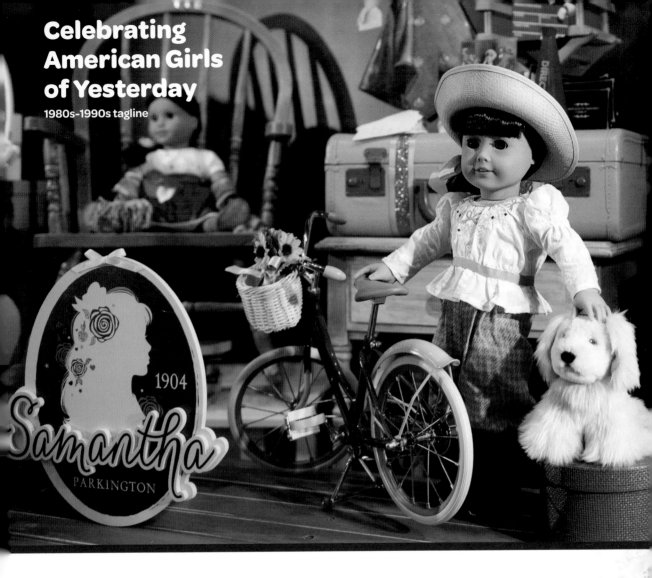

Celebrating American Girls of Yesterday

1980s-1990s tagline

Samantha PARKINGTON

1904

Over time, American Girl has released more than 15 historical dolls. Each doll represents a time in American history. For example, Felicity Merriman lived during the **Revolutionary War** in the late 1700s. Addy Walker escaped **slavery** during the **Civil War**.

Today, the line of historical dolls is called BeForever. These characters include older dolls such as Samantha and Addy. Others, such as Maryellen Larkin and Melody Ellison, are recent additions. Clothes and accessories are true to the times of the characters.

Each character has a series of books that tells the story of her life. The girls face many challenges. But eventually, each discovers what matters most to them. The BeForever line also includes thrilling mysteries and the My Journey books. My Journey books are about modern-day girls who travel back in time and meet their favorite BeForever characters. They share adventures, solve problems, and find surprises along the way. Each My Journey book has a different ending based on decisions the reader makes!

Samantha Returns
Samantha Parkington was retired in 2009, but she rejoined the BeForever line in 2014.

BeForever Dolls

Name	Release Year	Time Period
Addy	1993	1860s
Josefina	1997	1820s
Julie	2007	1970s
Kaya	2002	1760s
Kit	2000	1930s
Maryellen	2015	1950s
Melody	2016	1960s
Rebecca	2009	1910s
Samantha	2014	1900s

Addy

Kit

Julie

Expanding the Brand

Over time, American Girl included non-historical dolls. A line of baby dolls called Bitty Baby was released in 1995. They are smaller than full-sized American Girl dolls. This makes them easier for young children to handle. In 2016, American Girl introduced a new line called WellieWishers for ages 5 to 7. The line features a group of friends learning life lessons.

Little Girls, Big Hearts

2010s tagline

Chrissa Stands Strong actress Sammi Hanratty with Chrissa doll

A popular line called Girl of the Year was introduced in 2001. Since then, a new doll is released every year and the doll it replaces is **retired**. These characters are about 10 years old and live in modern times. Each uses her unique interests to make a difference in the world. The Girl of the Year collection also includes movies, books, and online games. In 2016, American Girl teamed up with Mega Bloks to make construction toys. They feature Girl of the Year characters and themed play sets.

American Girl also offers a line where kids can choose the appearance of their dolls. In 1995, this was introduced as the American Girl of Today line. It included 20 dolls with a variety of looks. Over the years, the line's name changed several times. Today, it is called Truly Me. Kids choose from about 40 Truly Me combinations. The dolls have different eye, skin, and hair colors. Some dolls even have freckles! Girls can add braces, earrings, or glasses.

She's just like you. You're a part of history, too.

1990s American Girl of Today tagline

Truly Me dolls also come with card sets. The cards give ideas for activities kids can do with their dolls, such as crafts, recipes, and quizzes. There are also Truly Me **apps**, as well as games and videos on the American Girl web site.

All Dolls Included

American Girl makes hearing aids, wheelchairs, crutches, and other specialized items for its dolls. The company also makes a Truly Me doll without hair for girls with hair loss.

Staying Connected

Today, large American Girl Place stores are located across the country. Stores are also open in Mexico and Canada. All stores sell dolls, clothes, and accessories. Larger stores offer other services, too. Kids design outfits and backpacks for their dolls on **tablets**. Stylists brush, curl, and braid doll hair at the doll salon. They can also pierce dolls' ears or fit them with hearing aids. A café serves snacks and drinks to guests and their dolls. Many stores also host birthday parties. Guests enjoy games, snacks, and birthday cake. Kids without dolls can borrow one from the store!

doll salon

Children stay connected to American Girl in other ways, too. American Girl's popular advice and activity books help girls navigate the ups and downs of growing up. *American Girl* magazine is aimed at kids ages 8 to 12. It includes articles, stories, puzzles, and advice. Today, it is one of the top children's magazines in the country.

Doll Doctors

Dolls in need of repair or cleaning are sent to the American Girl Doll Hospital in Middleton, Wisconsin. There, doll doctors replace bodies, heads, eyes, arms, and legs.

American Girl Gives Back

American Girl is committed to helping people in need. The company donates money, clothes, and books to a variety of **charitable** organizations. These donations are used to improve children's lives and promote **literacy**. The company also donates dolls to children's hospitals and libraries. They help bring comfort and smiles to children. Over time, American Girl has given more than $100 million in money and products.

The company also makes a difference with the Girl of the Year line. It holds events to raise money for causes that relate to the characters' stories. For example, Grace, a baker, inspired a program that raised money to help end child hunger. In other years, money was raised to protect **endangered** animals and support programs that stop bullying. American Girl helps children learn about the past and present with each doll!

American Girl Fashion Show benefiting Aubrey Rose Foundation

Fashion Shows
Some organizations have hosted American Girl Fashion Shows to raise money. These events featured kids and their dolls wearing historical and current clothes.

19

American Girl Timeline

1986
Pleasant Rowland launches Pleasant Company

1992
American Girl magazine is launched

1998
First American Girl Place opens

1996
American Girl web site is launched

2001
Lindsey Bergman, the first Girl of the Year doll, is introduced

1987
Historical fashions for girls are introduced

1995
American Girl of Today and Bitty Baby dolls are introduced

1998
Mattel buys Pleasant Company

2000
Pleasant Rowland retires as president of Pleasant Company

★ American Girl®

2004

Pleasant Company is renamed American Girl

2014

American Girl launches the BeForever historical line

2009

Chrissa Stands Strong, the first Girl of the Year movie, comes out

2016

American Girl Mega Bloks come out

2015

The line of personalized dolls is renamed Truly Me

2004

First American Girl movie, *Samantha: An American Girl Holiday,* is released

2016

WellieWishers line is released

Glossary

accessories—things added to something else to make it more useful or attractive

apps—small, specialized programs downloaded onto smartphones and other mobile devices

brand—a category of products all made by the same company

charitable—helping others in need

Civil War—the war fought in the United States between northern and southern states from 1861 to 1865

colonial—the look of European colonies in America in the 1600s and 1700s

endangered—at risk of becoming extinct

founder—a person who created a company

headquarters—a company's main office

literacy—the ability to read and write

logo—a symbol or design that identifies a brand or product

retired—no longer made available

Revolutionary War—the war for American independence fought between Great Britain and its American colonies from 1775 to 1783

slavery—a situation in which people are considered property; African Americans were bought and sold as slaves in the United States until the late 1800s.

tablets—handheld computers

To Learn More

AT THE LIBRARY

Anton, Carrie, Laurie Calkhoven, and Erin Falligant. *American Girl: Ultimate Visual Guide*. New York, N.Y.: DK Publishing, 2016.

Goddu, Krystyna Poray. *Dollmakers and Their Stories: Women Who Changed the World of Play*. New York, N.Y.: Henry Holt, 2004.

Green, Sara. *Barbie*. Minneapolis, Minn.: Bellwether Media, 2017.

ON THE WEB

Learning more about American Girl
is as easy as 1, 2, 3.

1. Go to www.factsurfer.com.

2. Enter "American Girl" into the search box.

3. Click the "Surf" button and you
   will see a list of related web sites.

With factsurfer.com, finding more information
is just a click away.

Index

The images in this book are reproduced through the courtesy of: Brian McEntire, front cover (center doll); Vince Yoong, front cover (books, top right center doll, dog), pp. 4 (books), 8 (book), 10, 20 (bottom left), 21 (bottom); Bellwether Media, front cover (blue shirt, shoes, green dress); walter sedriks/ Flickr, front cover (top right doll); tishomir, front cover (star); InSapphoWeTrust/ Flickr, front cover (top left center doll); Chelsea/ Flickr, front cover (top left doll); American Girl, LLC/ Wikipedia, pp. 3 (logo), 4 (logo), 20 (logo); Egomezta, pp. 5 (store), 20 (top); AlinaMD, p. 5 (background); Brendan Smialowski/ Getty Images, p. 7; Jennifer Szymaszek/ AP Images, p. 8 (photo bubble); Helen Session/ Alamy, p. 9; Ted Thai/ Getty Images, p. 11 (left); Jim, the Photographer/ Flickr, p. 11 (center left); dov makabaw sundry/ Alamy, pp. 11 (center right, right), 12; Everett Collection Inc/ Alamy, pp. 13, 21 (top left); terren in Virginia/ Flickr, p. 14; KidStock/ Newscom, p. 15 (top); Mario Tama/ Getty Images, p. 15 (bottom); Bebeto Matthews/ AP Images, p. 16; Brendan Fitterer/ Newscom, p. 17 (top); E. Jason Wambsgans/ KRT/ Newscom, p. 17 (bottom); AkaiKaze/ Wikipedia, p. 18; Sasha Parker-Cochran/ Aubrey Rose Foundation, p. 19; Steven Depolo/ Flickr, p. 21 (top right).